ALSO BY JOHN ASHBERY

PLANISPHERE

JOHN

NEW POEMS

ASHBERY

PLANISPHERE

ecco

An Imprint of HarperCollinsPublishers

HARPERCOLLINS BOOKS MAY BE PURCHASED FOR EDUCATIONAL,

BUSINESS, OR SALES PROMOTIONAL USE. FOR INFORMATION,

PLEASE WRITE: SPECIAL MARKETS DEPARTMENT, HARPERCOLLINS

PUBLISHERS, 10 EAST 53RD STREET, NEW YORK, NY 10022.

FIRST EDITION

DESIGNED AND COMPOSED BY QUEMADURA

PRINTED ON ACID-FREE PAPER

LIBRARY OF CONGRESS CATALOGING-IN-PUBLICATION DATA

IS AVAILABLE UPON REQUEST

ISBN: 978-0-06-191521-5

09 10 11 12 13 QK/RRD 10 9 8 7 6 5 4 3 2 1

FOR DAVID KERMANI

PLANISPHERE

ALCOVE

Is it possible that spring could be
once more approaching? We forget each time
what a mindless business it is, porous like sleep,
adrift on the horizon, refusing to take sides, "mugwump
of the final hour," lest an agenda—horrors!—be imputed to it,
and the whole point of its being spring collapse
like a hole dug in sand. It's breathy, though,
you have to say that for it.

And should further seasons coagulate
into years, like spilled, dried paint, why,
who's to say we weren't provident? We indeed
looked out for others as though they mattered, and they,
catching the spirit, came home with us, spent the night
in an alcove from which their breathing could be heard clearly.
But it's not over yet. Terrible incidents happen
daily. That's how we get around obstacles.

ATTABLED WITH

THE SPINNING YEARS

Does it mean one thing with work,
one with age, and so on?
Or are the two opposing doors
irrevocably closed? The song that started
in the middle, did that close down too?
Just because it says here I like tomatoes,
is that a reason to call off victory? Yet it says,
in such an understated way, that this is a small museum
of tints. I'm barely twenty-six, have been on Oprah
and such. The almost invisible blight
of the present bursts in on us. We walk
a little farther into the closeness we owned:
Surely that isn't snow? The leaves are still on the trees,
but they look wild suddenly.
I get up. *I guess I must be going.*

Not by a long shot in America. Tell us, Princess A-line,
tell us if you must, why is everything territorial?
It's OK, I don't mind. I never did. In a hundred years,
when today's modern buildings look inviting
again, like abstract bric-a-brac, we'll look back

at how we were cheated, pull up our socks, zip
our pants, then smile for the camera, watch
the birdie as he watches us all day.
His thematically undistinguished narrative gives no
cause for complaints, does one no favors
At night we crept back in, certain of acquittal
if not absolution, in God's good time, whose scalpel redeems us
even as the blip in His narrative makes us whole again.

Dreaming of Les Deux Magots in New England,
of spring before the drawn curtain of a snow shower,
I have to ask, why do these ideas circle me,
indifferent-seeming buzzards, and then the shock
of the told mysteriously comes to buttress me.

I dream of married couples having sex, shopping, everything,
and often get the giggles, staying here,
expecting something new to come along every five seconds.
That's new to me, I expect others will have heard about it.

Nonetheless one has to stay clamped
in simple ballet activity. The masters don't reign, yet by the same token,
they're not here, either. In order not to arouse suspicious
activity, pretend that conversation surrounds us like the air,
known, invisible. And sure enough
it's better out in back, around those self-forgetting trees.

BOULEVARD EXELMANS

IN THE RAIN

So many sad venues,
all the others in the house
will soon be leaving. "It's what
makes us stand."

"I won't be greedy tonight,
or generous. Just playful," he thinks
for the first time in years. "Flowers must
flourish, same as trees."

Next, permissions in the scary key
of E-flat minor, like Flemish bond,
interrupt the white-haired sage's
dreaming. I could do it all over
if I had to, he cautions.

High up under the roots the arguing
continues making its point.
The poultry bulbs made little noise.
A few rods away the word-bath
tacitly shoulders. Feelers sent out
tickled the always delicate negotiations.

BOUNDARY ISSUES

Here in life, they would understand.
How could it be otherwise? We had groped too,
unwise, till the margin began to give way,
at which point all was sullen, or lost, or both.

Now it was time, and there was nothing for it.

We had a good meal, I and my friend,
slurping from the milk pail, grabbing at newer vegetables.
Yet life was a desert. Come home, in good faith.
You can still decide to. But it wanted warmth.
Otherwise ruse and subtlety would become impossible
in the few years or hours left to us. "Yes, but . . ."
The iconic beggars shuffled off too. I told you,
once a breach emerges it will become a chasm
before anyone's had a chance to waver. A dispute
on the far side of town erupts into a war
in no time at all, and ends as abruptly. The tendency to heal
sweeps all before it, into the arroyo, the mineshaft,
into whatever pocket you were contemplating. And the truly lost
make up for it. It's always us that has to pay.

I have a suggestion to make: draw the sting out
as probingly as you please. Plaster the windows over

with wood pulp against the noon gloom proposing its enigmas,
its elixirs. Banish truth-telling.

That's the whole point, as I understand it.
Each new investigation rebuilds the urgency,
like a sand rampart. And further reflection undermines it,
causing its eventual collapse. We could see all that
from a distance, as on a curving abacus, in urgency mode
from day one, but by then dispatches hardly mattered.
It was camaraderie, or something like it, that did,
poring over us like we were papyri, hoping to find one
correct attitude sketched on the gaslit air, night's friendly takeover.

BREATHLIKE

Just as the day could use another hour,
I need another idea. Not a concept
or a slogan. Something more like a rut
made thousands of years ago by one of the first
wheels as it rolled along. It never came back
to see what it had done, and the rut
just stayed there, not thinking of itself
or calling attention to itself in any way.
Sun baked it. Water stood, or rather sat
in it. Wind covered it with dust, then blew it
away. Always it was available to itself
when it wished to be, which wasn't often.

Then there was a cup and ball theory
I told you about. A lot of people had left the coast.
Squirt conditions obtained. I forgot I overwhelmed you
once upon a time, between everybody's sound sleep
and waking afterward, trying to piece together
what had happened. The rut glimmered
through centuries of snow and after.
I suppose it was trying to make some point
but we never found out about that,
having come to know each other years later
when our interest in zoning had revived again.

THE BURNING CANDLE

That's what makes me feel that way.
A brief departure from the truth,
rejoining it up ahead: nothing to tell,
really. We grew up inside it.

I was dead wrong about that,
what the burning candle knew, confided
only to a few intimates. Then it was off
again, meaning on. Arguably, upstate

one of our business noses discerned
the flair, realized in a flash what the
consequences were, took the necessary
measures slowly. Then we

all knew what the awful thing would turn out to be,
how it would stay only briskly,
leaving not much of a souvenir behind.
Every face is that of a dinner guest.

Your generation doesn't have the propensity
to figure out light. It needs what it has—
colorful costumes, a lard sandwich. A "forgotten
elegance." It won't get better after this.

CHAIR RENTAL

Very little was known about anything
in the old time. It was as a vocalise
is to a sonata, children in the limelight
and water rushing over stones
as though in a hurry to get somewhere.
It's possible to joke about it now
that the trial period has lapsed.
To not admit you're miscast.

America's old churches were seen as a new
philosophy of one-upmanship:
playing, yet not part of the game.
Thus many things endure, and no one
gets very anxious about them: spots
like coins from a tree that who the heck
could have foreseen in its time anyway?
Just stand here. Call me potatoes
and soap. Call me soap and potatoes.

My husband's fiancée wished it otherwise.
There you go.

CIRCA

They were hunting debris in the grass.
It seemed that stencils of various types,
cut from many kinds of materials,
had existed in the not too remote past.

The problem was less what to do about it
than to escape responsibility for it.
They don't do it for you.
They had seen your brother-in-law until Sunday.

The joints within our model exhibited traces
of historical excitation. Days
with startling similarities in them.
There is one that you do not know
around all that. I'll admit to sleeping
at the side of the bed, a sordid boon.
The bastardly growing thing
would like us to get over the idea of number.

"It's false reasoning based on expectation,"
he admits. "Directed at a kind of pleasure principle
like bread." Having another crisis, worse times

than these, "we don't want the air in there too,
in her armpits crying."

You know something?
I don't care.

DECEMBRISTS

They met cute in the commissary, and for a while
it seemed as if it was going to be like old times
again. Then, as luck would have it,

they ruled him out, into a hole in Canada,
the air dense with no-see-ums,
applauded by no-goodniks. I mean it was awful

yet in a certain sense interesting—
the horizons, the atmospherics. By evening it
felt like we were all breathing easier.
A lake fanned out around the dock. Trestles
reported from far away, confirming good news

for many. And we, we lasted, as one lives in a tree
without thinking too much about it. You can't make
these things up, put a price on it. In microscopic,
supposedly disparate situations, he will be good
in just about everything he does, snooping,
giving us a chance to relax. How confident it was!
As recently as what seems like today we were mixing,

mixing it up, what a dismal friend of mine calls slurping,
eager to flip our leaders the bird.

Riffing brings us to odd headquarters.
Isn't that what a charmed life
is supposed to prevent, yet secretly encourage? He called
"Come up here." We grabbed another glimpse of
the books in the carrel, sweet in their stamped bindings.

DEEP SURPRISE

"LE PRESBYTÈRE N'A RIEN PERDU
DE SON CHARME NI LE JARDIN DE
SON ÉCLAT." —GASTON LEROUX,
LE MYSTÈRE DE LA CHAMBRE JAUNE

The beautiful lovers went away,
your eyewitnesses in the dance.

What is it you're starting to remember?
"My mistress' eyes are nothing like the sun,"

and I, in all weather, sought God's approval.
He "so loved" the earth that even I was stunned

for a few moments. And then, "Improve."
We were out for a fortnight and returned

to find the house, not ours, or different
in some inexplicable way. There's always

an indignant houseguest ghosting into them:
"Is that what they teach you in 'elementary' school?"

In my McGuffey's it says flower muscle
is believed to help. Seriously,

it's a definition and so much else. Or sleeping.
Parents agree. You'll love it big when you find out.

They were living in America at another time.
They were living in America for the FBI.
They were living in America shit wins.
They were living in America on the border with Canada.

They were living in America further gone into teats.
They were living in America that was the only good one.
They were living in America that was the only good one.
They were living in America who answers the phone and.

They were living in America deliriously.
They were living in America sadly.
They were living in America fictitiously.
They were living in America wedged.

They were living in America Stella by Starlight.
They were living in America the mighty sun.
They were living in America pandemically.
They were living in America across from the Ritz hotel.

They were living in America getting their chops.
They were living in America only for just one summer.
They were living in America beside the lake.
They were living in America for the defeatist troops.

They were living in America for the pleasure of it all.
They were living in America as well as can be expected.
They were living in America as one grows passionately
out of a love affair they were living there every day.

Does this doughnut remind you of a life preserver?
They were living in America to remind you of me.
They were living in America and a storm blew up suddenly.
They were living in America extended terms of credit.

They were living in America but it's all over.
They were living in America as tissue paper is to a comb.
They were living in America at fives and sixes.
They were living in America the same old same old.

EL DORADO

We have a friend in common, the retired sophomore.
His concern: that I shall get it like that,
in the right and righter of a green bush
chomping on future considerations. In the ghostly
dreams of others it appears I am all right,
and even going on tomorrow there is much
to be said on all these matters, "issues," like
"No rest for the weary." (And yet—why not?)
Feeling under orders is a way of showing up,
but stepping on Earth—she's not going to.
Ten shades of pleasing himself brings us to tomorrow
evening and will be back for more. I disagree
with you completely but couldn't be prouder
and fonder of you. So drink up. Feel good for two.

I do it in a lot of places. Subfusc El Dorado
is only one that I know something about.
Others are recently lost cities
where we used to live—they keep the names
we knew, sometimes. I do it in a lot of places.
Brash brats offer laughing advice,
as though anything I cared about could be difficult

or complicated now. That's the rub. Gusts of up
to forty-five miles an hour will be dropping in later
on tonight. No reason not to. So point at the luck
we know about. Living is a meatloaf sandwich.
I had a good time up there.

EPISODE

In old days, when they tried to figure out
how to write the sweetest melodies, they fell
on a bed, chewed the pillow. A moon rankled
in the crevices of a shutter. In 1935
the skirts were long and flared slightly,
suitably. Hats shaded part of the face.
Lipstick was fudgy and encouraging. There was
music in the names of the years. 1937
was welcoming too, though one bit one's lip
preparing for the pain that was sure to come.

"That must be awful." I was hoping you could
imagine it. Yet I will be articulate
again and articulate what we knew anyway
of what the lurching moon had taught us,
seeking music where there's something dumb being said.

And if it comes back to being all alone
at the starting gate, so be it. We hadn't wanted
this fuss, these extras. We were calm
under an appearance of turmoil, and so we remain
even today, an unwanted inspiration
to those who come immediately after

as well as those who came before, lots of them,
stretching back into times of discussion.
I told you so, we can handle it, hand on
the stick shift headed into a billboard
labeled Tomorrow, the adventures of new music,
melismas shrouding the past and the passing days.

EPISODE

or what's a heaven for?
which is yeastily

how jazzed we were
echoes of conspiracy

ran through it
the awful momentum

and doors will have to open
which doesn't mean it won't happen

meantime he does the prayers

the consequences of leaves
got thrown into a bath of lemon and eucalyptus
catalysts

the day was raging crisp
heavily outlined

he had been in touch with old buildings

Easy not to be a guest, you saw.
Hanging the paper perpendicular
to the wall was a lad's
night out. There was much else

about all that time too.
The water for it came around the corner
intimating ancientness and death
and so on. We don't allow much edge
because you see if anything
then we can't have the scenario
that would've looked good.

He still has a lot of money
for expenses, freebies
and the like. You don't want to teach them
milfoil, will grow out of it.
They can't in any case
purloin, bring something of it
back to the table.

Yet she continued to stay away
for several months, these

"the happiest of her career."
I didn't know nothing had
never happened there,
the decent story
you don't want to call.
We were imagining every situation
backing into us.
We were gone for a while. But it's not
too late. Who am I kidding.
The pond is a quilt, seen from far away.
The buttons are extras.

FLOATING AWAY

As virtuous men float mildly away
so do our minutes hasten toward the rain,
some speckled, some merely numinous,
and so it goes. The Traveler and his Shadow
find much to concur on. The wreckage of the sky
serves to confirm us in delicious error.
Congratulations on your life
anyway.
    Not even doing it
makes up for the loss it guaranteed.
Only a 28-year water supply
shields us from the desert.

Sticker shock awaits plaid gutter boys
pissing out over a stream. Surely if you were
going to count that against him the others would befall too.
That's not what he was saying, Uncle.
We're going to have a friendly chat with him
in the belief that someone will vote for you.

Pleated regret that is easier
by the end of the war inhibits only cats.

Some other holy man was here before
and the eunuchs made much over him.
In the small garden a harmonica was heard braying.

FOR FUCK'S SAKE

But it emerged dully further on
the what had happened a minute
digression or mild variation
on what had passed judgment.
There were a few, or rather, few
things to do to get ready.
Tie the little parcel of me
I may undo so as to tie it.
That's very nice.
Promise jokes. This is the cut hair,
the bloom that circles us.
If we enjoyed spring spells later
it was because the motoric finish
spalled. It isn't too grand.
There are other bird sufferers
amid wading stalks the tide left
as though forgotten. They come back.

THE FORESEEABLE FUTURE

And we just sat and dreamed, sailing around,
trying to force the sad living of friends,
of every spilled government day.

If I had perfect pitch would I notice
the buildup on that, behind hand?

Spray-on sex, he botanized.
That could never happen.

He's being held by Egyptian matrons.

FX

O in this bedsit I crave
expanded knowledge of the first click
bearpits o'erlook.
Why one day
matters more ne'er is told
O rats the scholar's rags
like a gypsy's take hold,
illuminate far tracks.
If this were all, the Creator
must have left his notes in the car
or 'twixt the marge of star
of gravel—yet we seep on,
more's unlit, uncovered.
These first saplings blanched, alive
'twere to be so. Next, schoolboys' pants,
olive gesture, are so.
To smash the nexus, underemploy
the conjoining verb, were pursuits
less windily employed in population's
hugged areas, O gee
in phantasy's cool reign
to be dusted off one era
since, almighty droop, clusters
of almonds next the sizzling bean.

Has it been all like unto
a weird and wonderful intro,
or, divining blistered
rage into consciousness?
An early cane
dismembered and in attic
of lovely garage not have access to air conditioning?
Fie, let the brute pluck
from Buonarroti's palm
and lift o'er o'erweening sentry's
visitor's gaze. The gentry's
not on board with this one,
then let hawks lisp, poke
tumescence out of clay. Ahoy.

Try this, but only for a while.
If it works, you can be said to have lost nothing,
which is what winning is. Who can imagine
what you brought to the courtroom? What beautiful expertise?
The tragic, unquestioning, amusing love of youth
scares everybody up. I pull on my pants
over my underpants. Isn't night over yet?
Not really. In five months my service expires.
Then we shall be together always.

A GOOSE WALKS ALONG A PATH

Seriously, a lot of things are being unmolded
as polyhedrons. I fell in with the water.

Now go on with the story.
Just have it on the hill tomorrow.

There were five of us including Mrs. Owen.
They wondered why word had been phoned in

because they were in striking distance.
I mean let's face it this is another occasion

worth uncorking a case of blips for.
A downed tree could have put it better,

but the fetishists thought *they* had the right-of-way.
Till tomorrow then. Over to the house

this morning. That's how it's like,
blowing in with the whistles

and imagine ornery, as in hyenas.
No pants on me she confided.

THE GRACIOUS SILHOUETTE

OF ... WHAT?

The great
slid close to
Gosh it feels so good to
the floor again

white document
the college of distant singing.
be on
someone chanced.

In a moment it
down the tables.
sometimes it takes a
to pull out all the stops,
to our dimension,
of the life of
A suitable reliquary

was allowed
Someone said
moment of crisis
return us
nothing not love
plants and firemen.
for clam-sized citizens.

HALF-RIDERS

Oh all the sheaves are getting attended
                        to and the girth is right.
Then I have to start and say
with more *fish* at the door one is also more
                        responsive,
                        takes that in and
                        plays some more.
                        The wounded in their fens counter
                        we are a live tribe this season!

It then seemed to work all right.
        I put a comment in your glass, we
        were a pair somehow.
        It showed on the scoreboard,
        then we were at a loss for the night. You know
        how with some things you just let go, well
        that was one of those times.
Go out in the store and paint it. It hurts.
        Add to light, a feverish, new vexation
        now become part of time

        and all it grazes.

HAPPY AS THE SUN

We know these women from our post cards:
beautiful but inclined to blow away.

And after?

Frozen or correct?

And after:

fadeout. A bowl containing eggs.
Instead of having to stand,
back into the language melody.

After that came a break.

HE WHO LOVES AND RUNS AWAY

The bad news is the ship hasn't arrived;
the good news is it hasn't left yet.
It is still being loaded by natives with cone-shaped
hats on their heads. Here come the transistors,
bananas, durian (a fruit said to have a noxious smell),
baby bottles, photocopiers, and souvenirs,
such glorious ones! Nothing useful except key-chains,
lockets to be furnished, a ball to stuff with life.

Yet it's hard not to imagine the loss.
I think, though I can't be sure,
that all this is being added to my bill.
Woe betide us! We shall never pay,
though, not in a million years.
Everything is promise.

Too late we acted outside the rhymes required,
honest, God-fearing, ass-wearing blokes
eager to accept the hand that fate had dealt us
and play with it. Now, brown sorrow is the correct
livery for when we go out. It's important to
find a copy of the reproduction and send

or sell it back to them, "and with milk."
That was the nicest thing about them, happy birthday.

For it you got a mandate?
Because I like it better, here, near the core.
You are sitting on the sofa.
Have a glass of something.
You will hear a city.

I DIDN'T KNOW WHAT TIME IT WAS

Something always happens.
Tripping the circuit breaker
he had to leave early.

But always there is someone watching.

Back at the jelly farm
I don't even know how to talk to you.
He went quietly.

With grapes the bower is laden.
They dance and don't fade.
The radiant enterprise tickles
oval waters.

Midnight again.

Some of them learned to tell time in
the new century. Gradually they lost out
in time's free-for-all.

In time's free-for-all
something always happens.

The fire doctor in the jerk store
cautioned caution.

Always, someone is watching.

IDEA OF STEVE

Too bad I have this idea of him
based on someone else, named Matt
(another uncluttered name), whom I disliked
for no reason other than having once thought
he misprised me, which I didn't really believe. (Whew!)
This is getting complicated, like always.

Let's leave Steve at the wellhead of a dream,
where he belongs, and belongs also to others
who will make fun of him and gradually come to despise
themselves for doing so. He was a nice person and besides
didn't deserve our unremitting attention, though
his bumper stickers indicated otherwise. Susan was different.
Who dials the phone and is further gone into snow
than the mass of individuals could be? She is quiet now,
she too.

IN A WONDERFUL PLACE

A piece of one held out—
of useful packaging
and other tales
of men beyond the sunset, foreheads slumped

in strange appreciation.
Others, still at school, charily accepted
the premise that lay outside.
Poems, dream-dipped,

accosted certainty at fixed points along the way:
the land of No Can Do.

I spent years exhausting my good works
on the public, all for seconds.
Time to shut down colored alphabets'
flutter in the fresh breeze of autumn. It
draws like a rout. Or a treat.

IN ONE AFTERNOON

I told them I was leaving and they were all thrilled.
(A phenomenon I have often observed.) Sound more
interesting enough? "Sterling and buoyed" was the reply.

Her name is amber. Stop being so selective
and I will match garters with you in a plaid surround.
Ask under the tranquilizing rain (the slickest
monotony always the most enchanting) geared to

one of the lucky containments. Otherwise
whip your congress that you don't know anything about.
Periods of activity (sewn back together)
congratulated the mall. He's been extremely . . .

I kind of liked it though, the eyeblush at full
ocean complement, shreds and other coins assembled
there. Nobody knows where we're going to have them,
my next meal. Beating like a separate Indian.

Ow. In fact ouch.
I was just bothering over
these torpid interpretations you see
when, blessed by grass, I understood the signs
in the round. I felt dated,
much as my contemporaries did.
The clouds noticed.

To be off and running
the distance of a hilltop from old frame
buildings without whose lens no one
seems to understand. Nor can they
move inside when the season decrees sheen:
black yet morbid at the sunflower's
peaked center. Yes you know I
was saying that too. Blank testicles.

Sometimes if we listen without noticing
at the packed city's center other oblongs allude
to what the hotel dissipates.
There were onions at the triangular coated
basin at the center of all aligning
and shy tempests attuned to cottage

meanderings—I mean, save me,
I might not have candle power
to unstring meritable hoops. I say,
have we no thin power rotting
in English kitchens for the duke's children
to inherit like insecure boats
too distant from the onyx horizon?

JUST HOW CLOUDY

EVERYTHING GETS

The ballast has shrunk
less than 30,000 days before the divvying up
of items and posthumous, other
handles of today's version of the truth.
The enamel is just not going to keep.
But wait, there's more:
I had not made a snug choice,
but was reproved by robbers.
I didn't find out a lot more later.
Not by a long chalk. He said he saw you
coming out of the hotel this afternoon. Said
he'd like to see you. Nuance or nuisance,
the judges weren't bowled over,
not this time. Refusing to admit
something is the matter with you is like taking
a life. There are no witnesses.
The wind rolls free. My summer Pontiac
expired high up on the slope, death found desirable
between your two stalwart legs.

Why does he like the lights that way,
adjusted for inflation? But by the standards

of an earlier, seemingly more bendable time,
all is chasm and not getting recorded
now or ever, admits that it's more tolerable.

Make sense to you?
Makes sense to me.

THE LATER ME

shrinks from encounters with the earlier one,
you know, *that* one. The one we don't speak about
except occasionally between Thanksgiving and New Year's.

A long time plotting, and he's written out
of the sequel. We gave him a pleasant death.
Maybe he'll be back soon,

we hope not. The china is all converted,
so we can dress together. Why a meeting was
never convened until yesterday remains unexplained,

along with much else. We thought it was tears.
Sitting alone in an open boat tells you a lot
about discipline. Any wrongdoing will be overlooked or punished.

Furthermore, Mr. Tuttle used to have to run in the streets.
Now, each time friendship happens, they're fully booked.
Sporting with Amaryllis in the shade is all fine and good,
but when your sparring partner gets there first
you wonder if it was all worth it. "Yes, why do it?"
I'm on hold. It will take quite a lot for this music
to grow on me. I meant no harm. I've helped him
from getting stuck before. Dumb thing. All my appetites are friendly.
Children too are free to go and come as they please.
I ask you only to choose between us, then shut down this election.
But don't reveal too much of your hand at any given time.
Then up and pipes the major, leave the hand in,
or change the vows. The bold, enduring menace of courtship is upon us
like the plague, and none of us can say what trouble
will be precipitated once it has had its way with us.
Our home is marshland. After dinner was wraparound.
You got a tender little look at it.

Outside, it never did turn golden.

Like a dog, it mattered
some way on, and cancelled a bench
where I was distraught to lie.
In only that distance, other
sisters came to life, wry eve
unto holidays' dismay, that was over
a sheer time. We played and loved
the angular difference of chips
garnished by sun flood.
Mute testimonials poured out
and over and over the last day was won.

How now we often notice chatter
give way to ache, or ague.
Only a few sibilants clatter.
Against the debonair argument, who can pose?
A dastardly hymen, moments ago
gone into the tips of trees.
Water fell to its knees
and managed to make it totally original
behind the blind belt—whispers then murmurs.
O take sand and bait
away and knit a tartan with it
like baize or antonyms' spectral metronome.
Be short.

THE LOGISTICS

Then tomorrow? Then tomorrow.
We'll travel; the day
will be a scorcher. Some say.
Travel beyond the rocks
to a taped place
some will recognize,
others not so much,
some not at all—
what place is this?

To come back for a few hours to
a city of 20,800 people,
all good citizens,
stout in work in doing
washed over by a wave,
they keep ducking,
imagining.
It doesn't dovetail
with the middle of the beginning:
the time we lost
getting here,
the few friends
who stayed

with us,
faithful to the ends of fronds.
Some beginning they puked,
and, get us out of here,
we're magicians too!
Sorry—
it doesn't balance out,
the way they dressed,
and traveled
past the farthest signs,
in fact to explore,
as none then knew.

Sorry,
it's raining.
Even if you like the rain,

it's raining somewhere.
Nowhere you can see.
And the people? They've left too,
wedged in a fucking dream.

LONGING OF THE ACCORDS

"LIFE'S WHITE MACHINE" —JEFF CLARK

AND GEOFFREY G. O'BRIEN

We're all tenants, of one kind
or another: lodgers, proprietors,
houseguests. So what matters is
what matters for most of us.
We shrink in silken alarm
in the corridor—someone is coming?
But boa-clad ushers receive us.

We were told we were on message,
were the subject, or topic. In fact
it made a little difference

but not enough to disturb or quiet us.
Concluding, perhaps rightly, we
were of the one or other sort, you signed off.
It was OK to take everything,
though not to want it.

LOST SONNET

They grow up too fast
these days. Unassumingness
becomes unwieldy, the woods
a place to walk from briskly.
You say your cunning comportment
is artless? Well then so am I
for containing you, champ.
Your tracks are alive with new interest.

The trail always sees what's up ahead,
which is resistance. No tooth
or star contradicts what is made
and hard to screw up. Wash the guest's
feet, the aviator. Jack was his name
and we were like brothers, though we never knew each other.

MAGNETIC FLOWERS

Mountain fiddle-playing ought to have warned you
there was a goods train on track 2
and seven hostages in the basement.
What more can we do for ourselves here?
Larded with our own good intentions
one progresses toward the breeze
in the breezeway, falls aggressively silent
as a spectacular sunset in a well-known country.

Then it's a fig for all your conventions,
diktats, sundry violations. You would have made a better suitor
outside, pouring water into the fountain.
All is mixed up, the genders keep on blurring,
the blitzkrieg welcomes us
and sleep is its own reward.

Yet we got mileage out of so much shooing.
The cats are more poised. There is a decibel in each
crater, that calls you home, to the huge valley.
I wasn't pretending to say much.
We were in league I guess
with truth to the extent of the green nap.
Prisoners interviewed you and I swallowed

my conscience with my Sunday best,
falling all over my knees and shoes.
That's right. There were seventeen of us then.
Music of an almost sickening sweetness
bore down on us out of darkness. You perspired,
gave full throat to requisite longings.
Then you would feel better about it.
Just move on over a little, preserve
the key moment with nard in the cart. Point up
the hippest place in the world,

                              unusual as a star.

The mild stars shone for us,
moving toward the decorative fire escape,
seeking a tower to escape the sun
above the roiling city.

Surely it was for you and me.
The unexpectedness of our music
flooded us early. There were two ways about it.
Man abandoned by his hopes drums
a little life into the countryside.
Then the periods collapse.

From our rising up to our going down
everybody was nice. Favors overwhelmed us
for a little while. Days subsided as
patient crowds looked on. No space here
for losers, or even what passes as successful
in flyover states. In Fort Wayne rubber
cement was growing tacky, silhouettes criticized
their want of substance. Aida and Don José,
thoughtful along the parapet,
communicate. Do you chew gum?

I suppose so.
Do you believe in long engagements?

It'll be better.
A better day.

Yes and when all dreams come up
for renewal, wiser to seek the unknown
in the interior at its last address.
Familiarity like that is forged over decades
separating the silents from the talkies,
the savannah from the brush.
One was encouraged into intimacy. Ideas
started that way, like froth at first.
Then we flirted with something downhill.

NO EXTRAS

Other than that, why,
you see there's no permanent pavement
or wave to lock into.
You just keep ambling up the drive,
sleep-drenched, serenity on hold.

"Petty angst," she would say.
The awesome jitters of morning.
What's more, its horses know you.
Thunder along the esplanade
cutting up our hybrid town
to find good birth stuff and glasses.
The little vase was too close to the edge
of the shelf. A mouse could have knocked it off.
Elodie. A paste is made of 2 parts court plaster,
one part fenugreek, 3 oz. filtered water.
Reina. A pasteboard invitation ("bristol") would
be returned or answered, the decorative border
left hanging, a frame . . .

                    of questionable utility.

NO REASON NOT TO

Parents raising their voices and others
long to join the pilgrims' downward trek,
if only to see nothing at the end of the gorge.

The mayor too was languid,
some kind of monsieur,
failing to grasp the humor in the kiddies' spree.

And truth just kind of sails overhead
like a turkey vulture, on parenthetical wing,
empty as a cupboard.

Interrupt me (then)
with semi-elaborate everything,
spores left by a cloud seizure.
The block of flats will find then forget us.

In an hour, I'll be late.
Don't let it worry you—it
won't come near, and I'll
be out. You were excited
about that. Weren't you?
I'll have the silence of the mind—
washes over and it doesn't
pollute the dish?

We became fixtures,
appanages of the any, starting out
as though that were everything.
Then the fixtures idea
blows you off, it's too late
to stir, really?
You and brother among the acorns?
If so, how's this?
Would it rhyme after the legions pulled
in their horns, like it was supposed
to at some point create a canal
to itself? But I was unrestless,
unwilling to grant its spiky nature
to the effable and so consolidate

this most mundane of coups.
The coming on is whatever
it's about. Limbo was nice
after a while. One got on with
everybody, "paying guests,"
the viewer's idea
being of some, a going, concern.
At night there is popcorn
and concessions—the other kind—
and we're depressed
but involved as who could be
in that other—narrow—era,
the battle-drenched on a par
with the only newly subversive.
Insist we try again;
there was some sense in it
but only late. Later was too late.

NOT MY FAVORITE SHIRT

or even undershirt, zinging
on the grass. The happiest place in the world.
Why we could have tryouts then.
Those who made it got to be seen
a last time, like the fourth declension
where everything ended in *u*,
a relatively neglected vowel. Hats were blissful
then, the margins
a bit off.

Who will take a deeper interest
once these flowers have been gathered
and bound, perhaps for later reference?
Who will notice us then
as we were noticed once?

The fire is coming.
It says to wait.

O KNAVE

Don't forget to write!
Hopefully it's coming to pass even as we speak,
by which I intend variorum wish lists padded
with reeds and days, people like your mother
or others unlike your mother who have nothing
in common with you except to be like you
whom they never know. How rich with
possibilities this lakeside afternoon is!
Scissors decorating the walls' gules or argent,
and some distance away, Hessian soldier molds
or firedogs, queering the visitor,
who can stand no more, appetites maxed out.
I was going to say drop me off further
but you already knew
this was what we both wanted.
I'll close saying you'll meet me in your dreams.
Be polite and not too aggressive
and not a little inquisitive, boring steed.

OCCURRENCE

I remember I remember
the word "shovel."
A very young person
—their child—called.
Was it right to remember
all the time? I am
sailing like a sheet in a play.
Others are there.
A dish of scrambled eggs
calls out of a dream.
We intuit the sill as "alarm."
Nuthatches covet the sky's
lashes.

THE OLD JURISDICTION

With all these things, why do you care
what notes the baby sings? His fists are full of grass
today, tomorrow he will be deaf. Doctors
on my peninsula concede a happy future
for some of us, the elect and the chosen.
For the gummed masses it's the heartbreak
of sameness, as all lines flow together
in a picture that awaits sunset. Same
as you, I wandered a little farther
than we were supposed to, found too late
the limitations of living in a street.

By anyone's standards I was an uncertain thing.
Butterflies at night flew over and past me,
then turned around for a better view
than they were accustomed to. And me, well, I,
too wrapped in wind to notice the stone over there,
summoned the stranger with his suitcase.
Look, there are live things for each of us.
The planets promise to roll next time,
and the mad fixer amends his list.

PARTIAL CLEARING

Yesterday was the worst.
You know what I also intuit
is having not enough gravitas
to bring the storm to its
self-desired conclusion. I mean the way
rarebit fiends stumble on truths
in the disordered dreaming of multitudes:
something we can't and won't
turn to our account—"vested"
interests.

You know, this is just
where you don't care: the average
walk of citizen A to the corner
of a square where all gets lost in
mumblety-peg. Where the pickpockets get by,
but only just. And sand freezes in the gutters.

Looking out the window reveals
that the weather is or isn't about to change.
Forelocks will be tugged in a fortnight
and other appraisers add to the already vehement

heap of misunderstood and eagerly approved evaluations:
a coming out into spring after a winter of
carefully worded captions. A love like self-love
upgraded to "pastoral." Yes, easy does it,
always. What you see will be used against you.

A PENITENCE

The joints within you
still won't dance.
Why the intense outcome?

Diamonds for every budget
customize tattered spaces.
It's nothing more, nor less,
than a seeming apocalypse:
air filled with air.

Someone will come along
to take care of you,
polish the millions of you
talking slang, happy as a zoo.
And it was so nice,
these leg warmers,
or a casual fugue.

Someday it will be as it is remembered.
Hurry, interesting life.

PERNILLA

Please don't apologize for pissing me off, you were
probably right, and I was halfway out the door
anyway, the living room door, leading to the hall
and all it contains. How is it that things can get
shiny and be peeling simultaneously? Seriously, Pa,
we would have come over if we'd knowed
the combination for long, and then folks'd have pointed
toward us, miming birdsong and the like.
It was too short a time to have wrapped many pensées in
but we weren't blighted by that, near the tower.
One who calls in need out of the dusk fancied our
situation but we were not to be perturbed by that, only a little fluted
toward day's indisputable margin. I say, how do you
like it and the bills floating along beside it,
like baby ducks after the mother has moved on to some
important barrier that will rise up like a chapter heading
in later life, when all is pretty much paved over and weeds
have begun to take hold? I said, how long
do you expect it and us to go on nourishing
whatever it is we do nurture. Madness, you implied,
to get so near the torrent and not stumble,

taking all things together, and we do
do that, just don't advertise it.

                    Come back
another day and I'll have forms for you with the prices,
as well as samples held close to the waist. That sure was
fun the day we took our gum out and the trees lurched
overhead, it was almost like being in a storm with no
clouds around to blame it on. Yes, well, I imagined other
settings for our unease than this. Now I'm mortified.
No you're not, she says, pick up here
where it says lost and join the boys in the harbor,
whether they have water wings or not, just bare chest bones
boring through the gloom and you lean up against one
whose sister is in Arcady and it plops the question
just like that, you old so-and-so, and needs must begone
in any case, though the hour isn't urgent
and the land mass teeters once more, crashing
out of gloaming onto the floor near your heels.

Comb it wet through these otherwise days.
"Difficult" scenes emerge. What was so bad about perjury?
Think back to how it teased us.
We were raised alive for the behest of others.
Children unwind us, grown-ups cobble us
into their frescoes. Night is seen as becoming.
We love you! This from the heralds.

Alas it isn't as easy once again.
The old bike just lies there.
I shall have to do something . . .
In the meantime living resolves itself
into a dance. A cinema. More light.

THE PERSON OF

WHOM YOU SPEAK

was in this room recently.
Her husband later, a tall sprinkly man,
heavier than we like to see, caught up.
Really why is there shouting,

going every place, in some time?
That's for you to know and me to find out,
possibly. Why all the glad rags?

At times to a great time
someone will shrug and beaters
fan out. There is a note of irony
in their affection that comes round,
always, like clockwork,
yet the unexpected.

They intend to go from there to here.
They say, I am righteous. They are dreaming.

We didn't plan for the event but it's nice,
nice as always, though surprise is never what

it seems. Now they're walking back, talking, grinning. Weather is in cahoots.

Work, win, suffer some more.

Mysterious barricades, a headrest (of sorts),
boarded the train at Shinjuku junction
to the palpable consternation of
certain other rubberneckers already installed
in the observation car of their dreams. "It's so peaceful
on my pallet. I could just live here."
In a second the deadbeat returned with lunch tokens.
It had been meant to be sublime, but hell was
what it more specifically resembled. Remember
to hold the course and take two of everything. That way
if we make journey's end before the tracks expire
we'll have been found living in it—the deep magenta
sunset I mean.

There is nothing like putting off a journey
until the next convenient interruption swamps
onlookers and ticket holders alike. We all more or less
resembled one another, until that fatal day in 1861
when the walkways fell off the mountains and the spruces
spruced down. I mean it was unimaginable in a way.
You'll have to install a park with chairs and restrooms
for the weary and a simple but firm visitors' code
for it to be given out in your name and become a boon

to limp multitudes who thought you were somebody else
or didn't know what it was you did. But we'll stay clean,
by God, and when the tide of misinformation reaches
the first terrace, we'll know what to do: yell our heads off
and admit to no mistakes.

The land stretched away like jelly into a confused cleft.
All was yapping, the race having ended
before we arrived, with mixed results.
Nobody knew what they owed or how much credit
had been advanced, being incapable of niceties like buzzing
and herding fleas till the next shipment of analgesics arrived.
It was like forming signals out of loam when you were young
and too discouraged to care very much
about aftershocks or where the die ended up.
It was too smoky in the little kitchen garden or *potager*
to pay much mind to the rabbits and their plankton
dispensary. Something had been launched. We knew that.

THE PLYWOOD YEARS

Here in the open, love lies apart,
singing to its beads. How reflective is that?
Don't be such a goose, love said.
They'll tinsel you.

They came after me and in the end I was a sot.
They said on TV it didn't matter.
One fallen ice cube is left. The others go in.
So it was on your conscience the hangover happened?

You don't want to call.
Others than you are surfeited.
Bobby Burns said a rose is like no other,
neither is a lintel a blood-red reef.

They came and sat on the pier next to me.
I had piqued their curiosity
just like in the old days.
One spoke to a kitten. They shrugged.

I hadn't had the mirror experience in the hangar
yet. Those were all days tumbling over me like water,

like a scented caress. Then a bumble bee
gladdens earth with its silver sound.

We lived under tarpaper and ebony slats,
dragging one's feet across the floor.
Oh if you're going to then do it
advised the eggbeater. Time got left out of the equation.

POEM

The sun travels all day,
then falls down.

Let us use your shoes
as they have almost demonstrated.

From its inscrutable lap
a chicken with a wooden leg issues.

All these people are running around.
I wonder what they do in real time.

PRODUCT PLACEMENT

With all the de-emphasis I'd
expected the new bill
to be unbreakable. Like marble.
Instead: handheld
receivership. The party of
the second part clearly
endorsed the setup. Water rained
on water lately. It looks like
there's so much pretension
and heaviness. Let him talk
to the border.

It doesn't mean
that he would never do it.
You end up sweating,
photographing not too hard underwear.

PROGRAMMER

What kind of a nuthouse is this
Hansel wondered. Early, evidently,
yet what crumbs had led us to this door,
and where, or why, are nothing to me now.
Seldom do they diminish. Another time
every year who creeps and scrambles may read
if not divine. What makes everything today
so sexy, so friendly? It was a disaster in history,
one fine day. Anyway it was at long last,

no one clubbable came to the door.
An existence like a sea urchin's
is what I inherited. Avast. And in the twinkling
some of it belongs to others, and we love them
as herring love the sea. You tell them.
Make yourselves at home the witch said,
I'll only be a minute. The words "I live,
I fought," form like marbles in the mouth.

The regional farm district is shut.
It's all a bit orthodox, yet one says, so long,
it's a period. Like waiting for a cold to break.
Was it a dream?

In his hot little hand, a smiley face.
People fainted in those days,
gasping at the shock of the truth
or what passed for it. Indeed, they were torn,
of two minds, over what constituted it,
which didn't prevent them from sitting down
and lecturing you about it. One thought it
all stemmed from his childhood, site
of an unwise maneuver that no one living
remembered anymore. He grieved like a citizen
grieving taxes. Not much came of it.

Others felt the secret was in the dance
or the weather. Both were too close
and mattered too much to get the job done.
Still, he knew no refund would result
from concerns conveyed to the courtroom
like that. Or any other way. It was a shame
the job had to get done,
especially when it was so nice outside.

REGO PARK

Whether now
or in a minute
he goes to bed—
the park fixtures supple
without.
The man stands at his stand
all day, twins
run about
as though looking for the
thing that will unlock
this—

Come away,
better to find
the back rack
if the adept blocker roils
sweet communion of sun
and fun

wherever others pass.
Cramped now,
college reunion of the
past—they walk through,

others smiling, defeated
on the first earth cycle.
So why give
courage to the blighted,
pass the additional costs
of waiting around that much
to the learned numskull
statistician—
or else why

choose what others choose?

RIVER OF THE CANOEFISH

These wilds came naturally by their monicker.
In 1825 the first canoefish was seen hanging offshore.
A few years later another one was spotted.
Today they are abundant as mackerel, as far as the eye can see,
tumbled, tumescent, tinted all the colors of the rainbow
though not in the same order,
a swelling, scumbled mass, rife with incident
and generally immune to sorrow.

Shall we gather at the river? On second thought, let's not.

THE SALVE MERCHANT

The seventh generation has it good,
if surprised sublimity's your bag (which
hopefully it is). The merchant testifies
to long commerce between you two:
feathers, flowers, subtle array of fruit,
and lesser hand-me-downs of nature.

Most likely you and I were wedged
in a romantic corner, and delivered a sigh,
as black evening arrived on time.

What were going to be the consequences
of waiting all day for the consequences
and then, like a girl with a hoop, changing
the subject to moist, glorious second thoughts?

The mother stood by. Others pretended not to hear
or not to notice. An aviary of perfectly OK ripostes
waltzed it around and became almost
monumental. Our consensus was rubies.

"I knew you were going to say that,"
somebody yelled at me. If this was what being justified

was like I was ready to play
or stop playing—it comes to the same thing.
Better to win not playing than be cheated
of pictures that were conveyable to you anyway.

SEMI-DETACHED

Red man gave me a pass. I should
have shunted, back there. Or maybe
closed my mouth? Don't see that.
Sanctimonious fraud, am I? Pharisee,
whited sepulcher, mealymouth, poseur;
"a saint abroad and a devil at home"?
Brr, why would anyone want to associate
with me, anyone in his "right mind"?
Then I remember, that to be popular
you have to have "poise." Well, that does it,
I'm outta here. Novices are more cunning
than I, who when I pause at the door,
pretending to stalk someone through the potted
palms, fizzle or peter or poop out.

When someone calls me by name it's always
a case of mistaken identity, a ringer.
On the other hand would I have waited while
the contretemps was sorted out? Not likely.
So it's off to the circus for us, you and me.
You'll never be more agitated than you are now,
at this insurpassable moment. I, on the other hand
am cool for the time being. Such is my creed.

THE SEVENTH CHIHUAHUA

This association item will tide you over
until the next blue January wind comes along
looking for space, and death.

The burgs (as in Harrisburg, St. Petersburg)
will accompany you part of the way,
then turn back, letting us feel their niceness.

Alongside, something was running.
It had a note in its maw. Hey,
give me that, like a good animal.
That's fine. Now get lost.

It was all about being on the way.
There were no addresses, only heavenly wings.
Did I say the stars will take care of us? I know

it sounds funny, but that's the way it is.

SLEEPINGLY

In a whole lot of ways the unique
drizzle isn't over it's tied to your side
while we enumerate pets and animals.

Close it down urges the governor.
Forget the painter's pants he got the
far side of the bargain anyway.
We're all strangers in here we can't see,

his magic crotch winging away
in time for school of, was it,
a distant lawn that spat the wind
out of my sails. How many, how far
do we have to get along with this
thing on our necks? Not since you came along

has there been so much slogging outside and in.
We're combing the area.
Bound to be more tips whatever fellas.
This mode I choose talks back.

We had just about decided about life,
a factitious mess you urged, and I, enthused,

pored over new books from the store.
Or else dispatch hassles, she being star
with lemon in her car
walking on a par
cheapskate missiles hurled
from one garden to the next
is what we're all about.

I mean how little can you toss off
and be ready for the rest of tomorrow's dense
armillary?

SOME HAD LUNCH

All this random money, committed money—
let me ask you this:
where's the self-indulgence in forgery,
fakery, if it doesn't get you in free,
past the momentarily distracted
ticket taker
who thinks she has seen you in a dream
eleven years ago? Why not just say that?

He put his foot down.
Last Sunday came an "aha" moment.
It would have told him of the hour
if he had waited . . .

But, see, nothing comes of it.
We can't forget everything,
and the boy stands at attention, distracted,
in the sexual chapel surrounded
by correct, cream-colored leaves. Others will benefit
from your ritual cleansing, as they have before,
and can go on ahead.

SOME SILLY THING

It's so confusing these days,
what with the activity and the fuss, flurry,
fluster, what have you. I'm in sympathy more
with the elves and you, good, hospitable
demons we can cherish with. At least
in those times was the flour and salt of difference,
liquor of misunderstanding the baby's presence
withdrew. Some of us were born fooling around
to be captured later in life and classified.
More of us played the fingerboard. Then there were the oval tops
spinning away as though their lives depended on it.
What other streets made such an impression
and why? Why did some stand out or read
as darker while others registered as pale and correct?
The truth is nobody knows what is happening anymore.
I for one am not sure it's a mistake
to go crackling on like this, with parents in a tizzy
and royal figurines registering disapproval.
What if there never was an infinite series
bisecting one's own orchard? Would that help?
And if the silent reading and the listening coincided
in a bellicose fraction this side of miscellany, would

they be confiscated any sooner? To the contrary, I believe
we are just this side of an enormous breakthrough,
that the captain knows about us and is on his way over.

Similarly in the last century you would see feedback
degenerating into laissez-faire. It was nice for those who lived then,
but few would want to be part of the rival solution
even if it left them breathless and on the edge of a forest
in a gothic novel. And then there was all the turning out all right
to be commandeered and somehow exploited for one's own narrative
off of whose dregs we are still living today.
Wilde said that history is merely gossip.
To that, add that portraiture is what a dressmaker's dummy feels
about today's hiatus or harvest, whenever bands of light
or shadow have taken over. Honestly, we're good with that.
It's like dawn in this globular attic room, one's inmost thoughts
to be breathed upon and revived like flowers, again and again.

SOMETHING IT WASN'T

Better homes and gardens for many
but for the rest, we are not so sure.
We need a place to turn around and be unctuous
in, feeling it not as a lack but
as something to be warded off. We are
not done with shoe polish yet
in a way we are. Isn't that inventiveness
or something coercive like a lash that cracks
close to the cheek, something you give back
after keeping it for a while?

As sure as there are servants in heaven
others will come up to you and ask what it was
you did today, whether nests were full
and anxious, and what kind of sun sprayed
on the corners of a cheap notebook
to be dreamed as all things are, except
for fountains and animals lisping kind losses,
fervent, over here. The way it is right now.

The playoffs—don't get upset.
What a process brothering it,
like a bottle of lemonade.
Your beautiful work doesn't coincide.

Where are the flurries, faked orgasms,
the glass texture? The spa, corrupt,
dead like a geranium
in the crosshairs at the end of time . . .

Was he young? Blond chimneys and a sense of
morning when it arrives. But was something
else expected of us, that could never be forbidden,
never forgotten? The push-pull of a city
drawn closer on wires? Sweet wood
floating on the sea?

A sense of cracks which may not become too noticeable
alerted them outside. No point coming back in,
the gap has been bridged. Around us, alarming as snow,
the troops "fall in." Everything is normal.
I can still scratch my head if I choose.

At stake is a page in some larger history,
something we had once and played with.
The laboratory seemed too kind, deliberate
for the miles of homecoming that were ours.

SONS OF THE DESERT

There is a tremendous interest in dog-related items,
such as dog-paintings. Once they figured out how to print on tin,
copper and silver with the horn on it,
you have all the written equipment. Really major, I'd say.
The lucky trees signed on. Then there was no room for latecomers.

He was a very mobile person throughout his life,
instrumental in helping promote the Indians.
Those escapements, they would use in their luaus.
It was my first ¾ length child. (Fumed oak.)
Look how funny her little arm is.

I think there's a big old lake.
I think the whole thing might be flooded by now
for reasons not fully understood.

This is how curious. Some stuff got in from the terrace
and peed on common sense. This is how my days,
my nights are spent, in a crowded vacuum
overlooking last year's sinkhole. What I was about to say . . .
Oh forget it. The weather is untenable. I'll be on my way.

So spake an irritable urchin
to nothing in particular. Come on, I'll race you to the corner.
Nothing doing, he said, my calluses
are in an uproar. Besides, we had an agreement. Oh really? Yes,
about the triathlon. You were going to save me
at the end, take me home with you, feed me
tea and toasted cheese, tell me stories about a race of Titans
who once lived in these parts. Oh, if that's all . . .

So began a curious kind of friendship.
I saw him only twice more
before his untimely but merciful death.
Both times he said, What about the cheese?

STICKER SHOCK

Such an unattractive idea,
yet we must pick it up, sniff it,
and put it aside, next to the penny
the maid left in the ashtray
so that I'll know she's honest.
Well, it *was* nice of her and I'd
trust her with lots more than a penny,
I know that. Speaking of which it's
nice to know what other people know,
even if we can't be sure or trust them.

Summer is all about being a season.
I'm not sure I can take too much more
of it, but while it lasts I'm along
for the ride. I'd be a jerk
not to be especially since there's no
alternative, it just keeps coming,
and we take it in, like a barn accepting
bales of hay from a hay wain, until
they're gone. That will have to do.
Besides (did I mention it?), I'm tired.
This day's a wrap. Others will happen along,
maybe fall in love with one. But that's another story.

We'll find a new wand, horizons will be bright
and anxious. A friend will give us
what we're owed and something extra,
something we couldn't have imagined,
a space like a dream.

STREET DUST

Put it on your child's calendar—
barring something like pizza,
horn failure, fairy vengeance, we can see
how quaint it was supposed to be.
Nothing gets under your skin like gravel,
dust, or apologies. These
we are called to witness.
The rest is nothing much,

yet belatedly comes to seem.
And then the tired depressed feelings life was expressing
stand in a new, modal sureness
of being seen, momently,
the drives spiralling out from under.
It's a tragedy that it's a loss,
hometowns unavailable.
There have been concerns, the often harrowing account
unanswerable for days,
overbearing. As leading questions reconstruct
a picture puzzle
the regional meaning comes to dominate
its near, farthest shore.
All the pieces belong.

Moonflower shimmers, a
kinder blur,
final as is a result.

Let old, new pets meet in neutral space.
Reunion fun outshines cruelty.

You don't see so much of these anymore,
not see so much of this. There were others
who saw more. Innocence is cool,
he offered. Now not so much.
Innocence is the finish. Through all our
wide day it stressed. It was foolish to argue,
idle to come undone. The post arrived.
It all failed. All failed somewhere.

STRUCTURES IN SAND

They still connect
(it still connects?)—
the feeling of the middle of the evening
as it is overtaken
by its sides.
And then everything must be taken up
and washed and put back together again.
Why is that so?
True happiness
(which we can't have, while we are close to believing
in it) ordains it, depends on life that ends.

Do you have enough
to refer the thing on this thing,
of many spirits
and cartoons?
There was just as much of the world then,
but it was distributed
less evenly.
Rome was closer than Canossa,
the old king dead,
dangling from mistletoe.

Breeze sends us back
to house.
Having been warned we strike
the new mission.
When are you returning?

THE STUMMING

I said I hadn't said it, he stressed.
What about poisonous sea snakes?
I know one. I bet you do. You
can be cute for only so long.
Then it's back to basics, or in
my case forensics. What doesn't
dapple you makes you strong.
Surely he'd have liked to know about that,
and where the insects go
when they sleep. As in a Telemann arpeggio,
one tooth very much resembles another tooth.

What one rear door does
is love's lament, her old sweet song
come on us brash in the early days,
tripping over a root but checking in
with the adorable lodgers. I felt it
in my attic. Combed the brush for suitable
attitudes and tints until it felt no more
no less than trough adjustment
at corners not meant to be revived.
Or ask Leporello. It's ashes and mesh.

SUMMER READING

With these lighter days a concomitant
urge to scrutiny arrives. Signing in,
my motivation palls, pusillanimous.
Are we to take it inside the house?
I have to go.

Tell me another dream. The long events surface
wider, farther apart, like autumn breakers.
Birds are suddenly there. The house of cards
on sand falters, fatally. I'm elated.

You never know how things work out
except through "sleight" of hand, sometimes.
I'm worried about knowing later.
The high-school principal killed his star student,

for instance. Feeling competent,
they quashed him. Until he wins the crisis
we can't promote it. Keep that rodent away.
What have you seemed to do?

Do interesting things well done and may
spring chasten you. We had everything in mind.
Everything softballed, wound up on my back porch.
It's okay, though. Keep us on your docket. Cut through the . . .

SURPRISING ANNOUNCEMENT

Great to see you on Friday! The whole damn dynasty. And we got it.

You're telling me.

Not knowing what it is you have in mind
didn't mean anything,
drove all the others off a cliff into the sun.
Baked rebellion. And I guess I won't keep it on the dresser anymore.

These are quite capacious.
Does it seem warm to you?
No man is just an island.
Day-glitter
in the valley creases.

Only Lucy can see over you.
Pay 'em for a while.
Use the word "bewitches" in a sentence
in the scarecrow position.

What is Jenny wearing to the dance tonight?
Seek alternate transportation.
Tag her remains.
Martyrs for a change

must be put to sleep,
midwinter savings, the years' income.
Have you noticed how far/long
the hairs in your nose don't take a day off from growing?
Chronology and ominous scribe complacency,
the pastel town dying
didn't mean anything,
will have an impact on horrified onlookers.

EAVESDROPPERS SELDOM HEAR GOOD OF THEMSELVES.

TESSERA

We had fallen asleep in the palace.
It was ungraceful, but only a kitten
could have taught us that, far out on a ledge.

The way some people come and go is instructive.
Why brood over shadows that pile up
inevitably inside the shutter? If there was
one thing he had learned in his life, it was this:
One discovery leads the way to another,
and then all are swept out with the morning's trash.

THEN THERE WAS THE

OCCASIONAL ABASEMENT

Sometimes the stars wiggled.
Only rarely did the taillight wince.
The chair backs all giggled.

What may we do for you today?
It has been decreed that a new order, vast as grasslands,
shall visit our constituency, pooling comestibles.
There will be dancing at night and a secret talon.
Nobody comes up short over these gradients.

The morning of life is a great treasurer.
By noon the mood has expanded to span streets.
Gardens have opened out like sinkholes
and lunch brought to focus on the poor dapper man
who likes his weight where he finds it.

Not surprisingly none of us was prepared
for the alternate emergency. We cleaned out our lives
like desks and brought new stamps
to the head of the torrent. No one felt like weaving
after that.

THEY KNEW WHAT THEY WANTED

They all kissed the bride.
They all laughed.
They came from beyond space.
They came by night.

They came to a city.
They came to blow up America.
They came to rob Las Vegas.
They dare not love.

They died with their boots on.
They shoot horses, don't they?
They go boom.
They got me covered.

They flew alone.
They gave him a gun.
They just had to get married.
They live. They loved life.

They live by night.
They drive by night.
They knew Mr. Knight
They were expendable.

They met in Argentina.
They met in Bombay.
They met in the dark.
They might be giants.

They made me a fugitive.
They made me a criminal.
They only kill their masters.
They shall have music.

They were sisters.
They still call me Bruce.
They won't believe me.
They won't forget.

THIS INCREDIBLE TAPESTRY

opened all around us and for four days
the saints bled and the skies proclaimed aloha
until it was time for the newborn to go home.

After having done that she was restless
and apparently undecided so other candidates
stepped up to the plate. And there was rancor
and some little rejoicing. So what did the separate
partakers do, on sun-warmed turf? It was time to drink,
and drink they did until the heavens reopened
and the stars were raked into a pile. It is God's
doing, the godless whispered, and so it became right.

Sure, he toweled, if it is this
fair way that answers up to you, you may dismiss the vowels
because one does not remember the yak that does not immediately
remember one. One does not scan the roads for politeness
or contribute to the desert economy. And lo
what he said became true for everyone
on earth and there was no parallel imagining.

After that you can go back to groundwork,
as though she'd been doin' it. One of the biggest

recycling efforts ever undertaken in modern history.
But the solons wanted to know, why aren't you the subject
and where does she get off dictating our lesson.

Listen, children, one doesn't get over that;
not tomorrow, not easily, not in the salt air
of a recent busy season. It just reads that way.
Any jerk can take his clothes off; principals may bathe
if one person understands how it works.

So they went to bed. Other days could promise this now.
It was wrenched out of our hands, and felt good.

THIS LISTENER

This listener, and others, required changes, then more changes.
It's quite a story. Mechanically the men are there,
including those who "gave at the office."
Maniacally the feeding frenzy continues.
Now it's we who are in the crosshairs—
a kind of giving in.

To lop off part of it is to look at it.
This proves I can contradict myself,
which I may not do. Others look at you,
think all right, let him prove himself
if that's what he wants. I, however,
want no part in it. It's "fussy."
More than that, it's more than a little
overwrought. Here, take some of it away.
That's what I thought. Nothing remains.
Now add a little of itself, swirling in,
like highway robbers, beggars of life.
The true part of it is like tin.
Isn't the truth always cheesy?

Here, make it a little more like you.
They'll like you for it

if they ever find out.
All of you will bear some share
of blame in the outcome,
yet all of you are part of each other,
blameless, ambitious. Sullen as afternoon.
Wounded but not deeply. (Weeping
wound doesn't make any sense.)
They laughed to be the tide coming in.

(Give in I quite thought.)

TOUS LES REGRETZ

Don't hold your breath but
hold me responsible
for what happens after that.
If he hollers just keep walking
passively, hand with
peashooter in pocket.
Why what a lovely day/street/
blank canvas/pause/orb/
old person/new song/milestone/
caned seat this is! I think so.

Have to get up,
locked in the desert,
survived by uncles, what a
bill of goods! The gods grown

testy,
mired in dissonance
like the first days of the store.

Club owners dismayed
at the season's turf. Electrify three units,
you're down a quart. I had her

sitting on the tub. Enjoyed
watching local weather.
I happen to like math a lot, and
meteorology
involved math, so it
seemed like a perfect fit.
And when I got to college,
I loved it. Loved yard work,
when she's not watching the sky.

Attention wolf nothing:

There is so much else
about all of that time too,
done in trances on your land,
caved to you.
O fast paperhanger.

See doctors late in the day.

and say to you

isn't really a tower. It's a square
building with towers at each
of the four corners. In the thirties
they made a movie of it starring Boris Karloff
as Mord the executioner, who dabbled in torture.
A busy man was Mord. His boss, Richard the Third,
was demanding. Richard had no hump
on his back, but Boris had a club foot,
as though to make up for it. Richard drowned
the Duke of Clarence, whose name wasn't Clarence,
in a tub of malmsey, a sweet-tasting wine.
Clarence had stood in his way. Richard
was determined to kill all who stood in his way,
including the princes in the Tower, two
little boys, practically infants, the sons
of old Henry the Sixth, or maybe of
Richard's half brother, Edward,
played by Ian Hunter. Richard was played by
Basil Rathbone, who also played Sherlock Holmes.

The princes, also named Richard
and Edward, I believe, hadn't done anything.

They didn't deserve to be killed.
But then, none of them did, including old Henry
the Sixth, although he was quite dotty at the time.

Richard's bride was unlike the Queen
in the play *Richard III*. She was played by
Barbara O'Neil, who played Scarlett O'Hara's
mother in *Gone with the Wind*, though she wasn't old
enough to be. That's the way I remember it. Wait, she was
actually Edward's wife. Richard took
unto him the Lady Anne, who was
played by Nan Grey, though she actually
married Wyatt (John Sutton) after they escaped from
the Tower, or the Castle. In the end Richard
killed just about everybody, except Mord,
who got thrown off a cliff by somebody,
a fitting end to a miserable career.

TRESPASSING

Deaf people always hear what they're not supposed to,
as, This is perhaps a little irksome,
will get on your nerves, maybe.
They want us to see and hear
but the jolly man won't let them,
deliberately steered them off course.
O then why make a fuss, why deliver them
to the open air? You know all things are going to sag.
Just don't let them bother you too much
or drift, if that's what you want.

At noon and at midnight,
approach the galvanized front door
in a spirit of lisping experiment.
Imagine what life inside could be
while you are outside. On this tedious steppe.
Or the fevered last time
of bunk inspection.

In the event it won't go on the air
still other precautions will probably be taken.
Then I can be something I'm not,
part of a stronger race (always assuming there is a stronger race),

a richer environment for the next seven months
as the sun most diligently made out
in much more than thirteen-mile-an-hour winds,
generally devoted to him.

My love, how like you this?

Not much actually,
my gentle uninjured self replied.
If that's all there is to feeling a lot better
I'd rather take my chances, you know, on the ice
or on a farm. It fits together
and mostly for our benefit, if you let it happen
or think it can somehow happen, in somebody's yard.

UM

So we'll go no more a-teething.
For now. When the urge
to perambulation strikes, feeling
dulcet in your own happy home,
why we'll declare it unintelligible,
past, beyond belief.

Put another way, God is singular,
strong in feeling, wise in the ways of others.
His flesh is singular, like water,
His feeling anchored in a deep pool.
Get Him back.
He's on an eagle trip.

UNCHISELED,

wedged in that music,
storm's got his arms all over me.

Day
feels modest about her pubic hair.
Would like to move to some other street,
the honesty of late light there.
The ample chill petitions those who go about their business.

You came up and what were we listening to?
They came decidedly over me, Europe and Africa.
Why was I punished at all?
Something nomadic herdsmen knew,
a winter's tale, available to the curious
and the curious.
Something your night can tell you.

UPSTATE DANCERS

The plants grow in proscribed wonder
at having accomplished this feat,
at least this far. Ivy, calceolaria,
don't have that much to think about—
any and all distractions welcome.

As one would spear a fish
the next layer becomes rudely evident.
"All of us here"—including me out—
are eager to know your plans
and to help in any way we could.

Sometimes a stench decides everything.
We're all better at some things.
It doesn't matter that your soles have patches,
that your big toe wiggles appreciatively.
Some of us are going to mind more than others.

Upstate dancers don't dance much
anymore. The trolley line sped through,
shucks, an empire ago. Fishing lures
were coated with a sandy surface—makes 'em
more attractive I believe. So why did
it happen with an echo? We thought we
had taken it into account. Turns out we were wrong.

We were sitting there, and
I made a joke about how
it doesn't dovetail: time,
one minute running out
faster then the one in front
it catches up to.
That way, I said,
there can be no waste.
Waste is virtually eliminated.

To come back for a few hours to
the present subject, a painting,
looking like it was seen,
half turning around, slightly apprehensive,
but it has to pay attention
to what's up ahead: a vision.
Therefore poetry dissolves in
brilliant moisture and reads us
to us.
A faint notion. Too many words,
but precious.

I don't know, I favor a little more crispness
in the attack (as in "attack"). People are funny,
wherever you go shivers you. A stupor like sheep's nostrils
chases the ground. Day arrives with a thwack
and is left to sit all day.

Well I can't stay. I was meant to
follow people like you. Now it's done.
These are sacred conversations we are having.
Poetry is seriously out of joint.
Fakirs pursue us. Late for the banquet again!
Seriously how can you stand yourself
the way you are well that's the way I am.
We'll talk about it.
Sunset calms, soothes,
rain is toothsome,
and you get all out of debt like that.

They know so much more, and so much less,
"innocent details" and other. It was time to
put up or shut up. Claymation is so over,
the king thought. The watercolor virus
sidetracked tens.

Something tells me you'll be reading this on a train
stumbling through rural Georgia, wiping sleep
from your eyes as the conductor passes through
carrying a bun. We're moving today,
today on the couch.

VOICE-OVER

Here, as I have erected
mammoth flowers,
my final valentine
the
consequently overbaked
unusable labyrinth
of kisses
translates us to a nearer shore.

How hard to understand,
difficult, hard,
obscure, vague, indistinct,
this morning of so much light
with afternoon full on us,
treading water till night takes over.

Another person in a great deal of trouble
signals enough has been done
already,
tells us how time has shrunk
to almost-entity,
that barring unsieved foul matter

we are effluents, to do
as we chose,

and in a matter of time
halts
the comma, peels the tonsil
of the complete serenade.

Try these other flavors
in your country;
I hadn't been meaning to go on
about the slimness of our situation
here at Lost Borders.
Here as I have erected
to do is a baseball bat.
Thank you so much for letting me listen today.
You know how it bears
on the tidal wave, center
of the *offusqué* storm we
are starting to learn about.

We are the day of the book.
Knaves that came along,
fig-roasts in the fall
in film chatter came to the same
albeit different conclusion.

THE WINEMAKERS

It wasn't meant to stand for what it stood for.
Only a pup tent could do that. Besides, we were in a state
called New York, where only bees made sense.

Those who were with us were not with us
and deserved a spanking. Others, looking out
over the bay's mild waters could barely distinguish
a message made of logs: "Return to the frontier
or all is lost, though in time some may reap
the benefit and glory of a frozen attitude."
My mind was made up.
We would start for Illinois that very day.

Have you considered firecrackers?
The deft music contained therein
assuages all contenders. Those who arrive last
at the party receive the most intelligent door prizes.
My niece is in Nepal. My name was memorized
last week for the chilling rolls to come,
in which foot soldiers gasp, giggle, and dream.
Say this for warmer climes, though:
Bears are let out at night to patrol the streets.

In the morning hope flushes the city anew.
I guess it was just that I always thought of snow
at the wrong times and defeatism came charging through the barricades.
It always knew where to find me.

Funny, few can now remember how water
came in pails once, and sails were free
for anyone who needed them for a boat.
Besides this six different types of student
were always shackled to the end of the wharf
in case anybody could use them for anything.
I think there's a wind mask
out near the glue factory. So many kinds of hope
began the race. Some morphed into local interest
along the way; others discharged family and civic responsibilities.
Each of us was assigned a particular task, though none
realized it until the task was accomplished
and forgotten. The brouhaha of learning didn't
seem to affect some any more than it did their teachers,
by now asleep. Night was soft for that sort of thing.

You remember the one, the little electrical villages down the road.
I'll have a mustard coke. In ordinary times a store can find that.
Ah, but we live in a peculiar era.
You can't get from there to here.
Well, now it's something I'd be happy to write about.
It lands on your roof, a small package,
loved and warmed. For all your posturing you'd say so too,

I'd wager. Well, that's enough of that now.
Better stack our hats in the cloud chamber.

Her magical bracelet opened suddenly
as though it were Christmas. We'd better be getting along
before it gets dark, or there's no way out of the box.
They don't carry them anymore, besides which
there's not much interest, only songs of the night
and fruits so beautifully presented
you'd swear you were in Asia the time before
this one, whatever it is, or where we
fetched up in the last century, the recent one
I mean. Like a dance, it completed itself
and ran out. Hey, it was just here!

So it is with the things that were more or less
dear to us and are now enfolded in the dream
of their happening. A man comes to the end of the drive,
looks around. No one sees him. He putters
and in the end is the last to leave. We may write about him,
or how his walk affected us. There he goes
again. If tact is a mortal sin
we shall not miss.

Where is Rumpelstiltskin when we need him?
The glass is low,
the bard, weatherwise, who wrote
the grand old ballad of "Sir Patrick,"
comes on all queer.
Do you hear what's happening outside?

These days I bring the horoscope myself.
One can't be too careful,
a woman runs a terrible risk.
What I was going to ask you is . . . I forgot.
A frightened god "trims minds."

About fourteen passengers working overtime
by the end of the war restored challenged idées reçues,
set things to rights,
generated crossover buzz
with naked foot stalking my chamber . . .

WORLD'S LARGEST

GLASS OF WATER

Bunny and Squirrel couldn't believe
who it was they came after! No sun
at the orphanage, no proctors
in the veiled classroom. It wasn't
going to be like this at first. Somebody
must have flicked the wrong switch.

Now it was even later after that.
Trees in bloom ten years ago
added to the commotion. Along the roads
leading out of town, old people
bobbed and turned, as though stuck
in wet cement. Loafers turned up
on cue. Interestingly there was little
to comment on, as though the big newspaper
had blown through, scouring everything
in its dull path. I don't want to wait
for this month to come, Squirrel said.
The fountain is an underwater phoenix.

The harpsichord went all adventurous
just as I was taking in the laundry.

We'd been promised extra pinnacles
since April, but this is tragic.
I know I only came to be here a second,
then leave to send you more postcards
and letters. Run along, like a good thing.
Powder the axles, wish the dog happy birthday.
There's no time like a fuzzy present, she shared.

WULF

Is that a groin? The doctor was kind
but insistent keeping the shuttle in motion
until the thread ran out. Show me the right tree
and I'll bark up it, I said. But first remove these,
your minions, from the walkway
and breezeway. In a flash, it was done. The discovery
was finished. Then gentle it some more
until the commas fall in place, he urged.
Once more I was on the right trail, though indistinctness
was on the agenda. What about the right to vote for others,
I pressed. Just what is it
that makes them so delicious?

For a while the castes kept their distance.
The mighty shuffled to another section of the parterre.
Their macaronic self-absorption prevailed.
Soon it was time to choose another climate.
We all bathed willingly. The diving bell came apart at the seams.
And you know what? For a long time afterward, the world grew
chipper,
offering samples of itself to every comer.
That's why I was so late.
It takes a long time to choose
when you're not ready. Even longer when you are.
You know this better than anyone, myself included.

YOU HAVEN'T RECEIVED

THE LETTERS YET?

And you'll see how it goes.
Since the day in front of you
is a ring toss, what about other egresses?

Not looking presidential
is what it boils down to, I told you to
keep the pictures under your belt.

Or these words: how do you expect me
to imagine our plight if this room has no context?
We were here once before, that we can tell,

but otherwise all is madness and hushed
compliance. The dog goes along the wall,
it has finished for the day. Other tropes slow

us, action is a glimmer at the edge
of a well. We saw and thought so many things,
couldn't explain them even to witnesses,

charming as they were. In the end a piece of silk
is our reward, wide as a mountain's flank
and caked with curious chevrons.

ZERO PERCENTAGE

So call it untitled, but
don't imagine you'll be let off the hook:
The title will find it as surely
as a heat-seeking missile locks on
an asteroid. Down below, armies
and oceans of taxis will squawk unfeelingly.
The title always wins.

ZYMURGY

Downtown was a maze then.
All the wares looked half-hearted.
There was no lion to complain to.

Alphonse I of Bemidji
made it a decent pilgrimage.
Others were on the trail.

Nobody sticks a finger in an electric fan
to see what will happen. Conversely,
we have all we can think about.

More shame on the way
for the big man.
The acrostic lost its apples.

I was away then during a decade
that other lambs began to rule.
Not within a radius of forty miles

did the traveling salesman approach with his sheep.
It is all downhill,
wasn't it?

No but I'd like to talk to you about it
half-hurled from the farthest corner
of the shy room.

Goblins or Gobelins?
A little of both, thanks very much
and can stick another thing on it.

The American back is shy
of that other great white way,
the tainted head.

People,
you gonna know
you gonna do

you do something else.
Mais non, je t'adore.
Not a good day for the blueshirts,

I could then get it to you,
these—insane, mostly
causing victims light discomfort

The still-interested crept back in.
The younger football thanked it.
Life had been forgotten.

Love me anyway, he said.

The author gratefully acknowledges the following publications
in which poems in Planisphere first appeared, sometimes in slightly
different form: American Poetry Review, Boulevard Magenta, Conjunctions,
Lana Turner, London Review of Books, Margie, The Nation, The New York
Review of Books, The New Yorker, The Paris Review, PN Review, Poetry,
Raritan, The Times Literary Supplement, Vanitas, and Washington Square.

"In One Afternoon" was commissioned by the Port Authority of
New York and New Jersey and first published in A Poetic Celebration
of the Hudson River to commemorate the quadricentennial in 2009 of
Henry Hudson's discovery of the river that now bears his name.

"They Knew What They Wanted," a collage of movie titles,
was included in the catalogue of the same title published
in conjunction with an exhibition of John Ashbery's
collages at the Tibor de Nagy Gallery, New York City,
in September 2008 (www.tibordenagy.com).

For additional biographical and bibliographic
information, please visit the Web site of the Ashbery
Resource Center, a project of the Flow Chart Foundation,
at www.flowchartfoundation.org/arc.

On the following pages, a stanza break occurs
at the bottom of the page (not including pages on
which the break is evident because of the regular
stanzaic structure of the poem): 26, 39, 96.